LIVING
SOBER,
LIVING
FREE

A Guided Journal for Women
Who Want to Stop Drinking

MICHELLE
SMITH

CASTLE POINT BOOKS

NEW YORK

THIS JOURNAL BELONGS TO

_____

GIVING UP ONE
THING CAN BRING
ENDLESS
POSSIBILITIES.

INTRODUCTION

When we make the decision to stop drinking (whether for a break or for good), we often focus on what we're giving up. But a more powerful way to look at it may be to think about all that we have to gain! *Living Sober, Living Free* is designed to help you do just that. By journaling each day, you can set your intentions to:

- Take the best care of your body
- Build your mental and emotional strength
- Be fully present in your relationships and experiences
- Find healthy coping tools that work for you
- Reclaim your clarity and focus from alcohol

This is your time to live the life you truly want. *Living Sober, Living Free* can help you get there. Through the thoughtful prompts in this guided journal, you'll see what's working well and which areas in your life need some extra attention as you cut out drinking.

The most powerful change you may see is on the inside. In sobriety, one of the hardest things to contend with is what to do with the noise in your head. A journal gives you space to let go and find freedom. If your inner voice isn't building you up, set it straight. If your choices aren't taking you places you want to be, change them. Flush out what's not serving you while allowing space for new possibilities to lead you to a happier, healthier life.

To get the most out of your journaling experience:

MAKE IT A "BOOKEND" ROUTINE. Start your day with a check-in on how you're feeling, a reminder of all you gain by not drinking, and a gratitude moment to get in a good headspace for the day ahead. These are the first three prompts within the every-day journal pages of *Living Sober, Living Free*. Then come back to close your day with appreciation for any self-care steps you took, celebration of an accomplishment (no matter how seemingly small!), and an intention for the next day. You'll find that taking just a few minutes at the beginning and end of each day to shift your mindset is incredibly powerful.

SAY WHAT YOU NEED TO SAY. Don't worry about sounding nice or making words flow perfectly. Be raw and honest with yourself. You need to see the challenges to find ways through them.

ONLY TURN BACK TO MOVE FORWARD. Living in the past will get you nowhere. But reviewing previous struggles and seeing how you have overcome hurdles can give you new perspectives and confidence.

LOOK FOR PROGRESS, NOT PERFECTION. You'll soon see all the good adding up.

Keep at it and you'll find more beauty, peace, and contentment with each day of alcohol-free living. So let's dive in!

☀ HOW I'M FEELING RIGHT NOW:

☀ TODAY I'M NOT DRINKING BECAUSE . . .

I want to be my best.

 I'M GRATEFUL FOR . . .

1. Decreased anxiety
2. Sparkling water
3. My family

No is a complete sentence—you owe no one any reasons.

☾ I PRACTICED SELF-CARE BY . . .

1. Sleeping 8 hours
2. Drinking water
3. Getting out for a 30-min walk

☾ TODAY I ACCOMPLISHED . . .

Listening to a sober podcast

☾ TOMORROW I WILL FOCUS ON . . .

Improving the way I speak to myself

☀ HOW I'M FEELING RIGHT NOW:

☀ TODAY I'M NOT DRINKING BECAUSE . . .

☀ I'M GRATEFUL FOR . . .

1.

2.

3.

Setbacks are often part of the journey, but you never start
back at square one. You're starting from experience.

☾ I PRACTICED SELF-CARE BY . . .

1.

2.

3.

☾ TODAY I ACCOMPLISHED . . .

☾ TOMORROW I WILL FOCUS ON . . .

_____ / _____ / _____   _____ DAYS SOBER

☀ HOW I'M FEELING RIGHT NOW:

😄 🙂 😐 😢 😕 😌ᶻᶻ 😍 😶 😠 😟 🙂

☀ TODAY I'M NOT DRINKING BECAUSE . . .

☀ I'M GRATEFUL FOR . . .

    1.

    2.

    3.

>>> It's okay to end the day with water, not wine. <<<

☾ I PRACTICED SELF-CARE BY . . .

    1.

    2.

    3.

☾ TODAY I ACCOMPLISHED . . .

☾ TOMORROW I WILL FOCUS ON . . .

_____ / _____ / _____   _____ **DAYS SOBER**

 HOW I'M FEELING RIGHT NOW:

😊 🙂 😐 😢 😟 😴 😍 😕 😠 😬 🙂

 TODAY I'M NOT DRINKING BECAUSE . . .

 I'M GRATEFUL FOR . . .

1.

2.

3.

> Congratulate yourself for cutting out alcohol—
> one of the top three causes of preventable cancer.

 I PRACTICED SELF-CARE BY . . .

1.

2.

3.

 TODAY I ACCOMPLISHED . . .

 TOMORROW I WILL FOCUS ON . . .

NEVER FEEL GUILTY
ABOUT . . .

- Telling people no.
- Not responding to a text or an email right away.
- Outgrowing relationships.
- Standing by your values even when they're unpopular.
- Speaking up when something makes you uncomfortable.
- Not knowing the answer to every question.
- Your body.
- Your relationship status.
- Self-care.
- Knowing your worth.
- Living a clean and sober life.

- _____
- _____
- _____

Fill in any additional reminders you need.

☀ HOW I'M FEELING RIGHT NOW:

☀ TODAY I'M NOT DRINKING BECAUSE . . .

☀ I'M GRATEFUL FOR . . .

1.

2.

3.

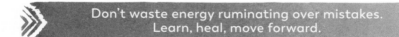

Don't waste energy ruminating over mistakes.
Learn, heal, move forward.

☾ I PRACTICED SELF-CARE BY . . .

1.

2.

3.

☾ TODAY I ACCOMPLISHED . . .

☾ TOMORROW I WILL FOCUS ON . . .

 HOW I'M FEELING RIGHT NOW:

 TODAY I'M NOT DRINKING BECAUSE . . .

I'M GRATEFUL FOR . . .

1.

2.

3.

> Sometimes the healthiest relationship with alcohol
> is no relationship at all.

🌙 **I PRACTICED SELF-CARE BY . . .**

1.

2.

3.

🌙 **TODAY I ACCOMPLISHED . . .**

🌙 **TOMORROW I WILL FOCUS ON . . .**

HOW I'M FEELING RIGHT NOW:

 TODAY I'M NOT DRINKING BECAUSE . . .

 I'M GRATEFUL FOR . . .

1.

2.

3.

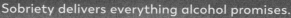 Sobriety delivers everything alcohol promises.

 I PRACTICED SELF-CARE BY . . .

1.

2.

3.

 TODAY I ACCOMPLISHED . . .

 TOMORROW I WILL FOCUS ON . . .

☀ HOW I'M FEELING RIGHT NOW:

☀ TODAY I'M NOT DRINKING BECAUSE . . .

☀ I'M GRATEFUL FOR . . .

   1.

   2.

   3.

Fill the space that cutting out alcohol has given you.
Schedule plans and activities, and take back your life.

☾ I PRACTICED SELF-CARE BY . . .

   1.

   2.

   3.

☾ TODAY I ACCOMPLISHED . . .

☾ TOMORROW I WILL FOCUS ON . . .

☀ HOW I'M FEELING RIGHT NOW:

☀ TODAY I'M NOT DRINKING BECAUSE . . .

☀ I'M GRATEFUL FOR . . .

1.

2.

3.

> Free your decisions from others' opinions.
> You know you best.

☾ I PRACTICED SELF-CARE BY . . .

1.

2.

3.

☾ TODAY I ACCOMPLISHED . . .

☾ TOMORROW I WILL FOCUS ON . . .

_____ / _____ / _____   _____ DAYS SOBER

☀ HOW I'M FEELING RIGHT NOW:

☀ TODAY I'M NOT DRINKING BECAUSE . . .

☀ I'M GRATEFUL FOR . . .

1.

2.

3.

> Be the reason someone believes sobriety is possible.

☾ I PRACTICED SELF-CARE BY . . .

1.

2.

3.

☾ TODAY I ACCOMPLISHED . . .

☾ TOMORROW I WILL FOCUS ON . . .

KNOW THE TRUTH

TRUE ⟶ **ALSO TRUE**

The peer pressure ⟶ Your boundaries
is real. strengthen.

The cravings ⟶ Your cravings
are intense. diminish.

The vulnerability ⟶ Your vulnerability becomes
is terrifying. someone else's survival guide.

The strength ⟶ Your strength
is exhausting. becomes infectious.

The noise is loud. ⟶ Your mind becomes
confident.

_____ ⟶ _____

_____ ⟶ _____

Fill in any additional truths that you are learning.

_____ / _____ / _____   _____ DAYS SOBER

☀ HOW I'M FEELING RIGHT NOW:

😀 🙂 😐 🙁 😟 😌ᶻ 😍 😐 😠 😰 🙂

☀ TODAY I'M NOT DRINKING BECAUSE . . .

☀ I'M GRATEFUL FOR . . .

1.

2.

3.

> You don't have to hit some type of rock bottom to ditch something that doesn't serve you.

☾ I PRACTICED SELF-CARE BY . . .

1.

2.

3.

☾ TODAY I ACCOMPLISHED . . .

☾ TOMORROW I WILL FOCUS ON . . .

☀ HOW I'M FEELING RIGHT NOW:

😄 🙂 😐 😢 😟 😌 😍 😐 😣 😖 🙂

☀ TODAY I'M NOT DRINKING BECAUSE . . .

☀ I'M GRATEFUL FOR . . .

1.

2.

3.

>>> There is no perfect time to start sobriety.
Give yourself permission to start messy. <<<

☾ I PRACTICED SELF-CARE BY . . .

1.

2.

3.

☾ TODAY I ACCOMPLISHED . . .

☾ TOMORROW I WILL FOCUS ON . . .

HOW I'M FEELING RIGHT NOW:

 TODAY I'M NOT DRINKING BECAUSE . . .

 I'M GRATEFUL FOR . . .

1.

2.

3.

> Love yourself through the curiosity of learning where alcohol fits into your life.

 I PRACTICED SELF-CARE BY . . .

1.

2.

3.

 TODAY I ACCOMPLISHED . . .

 TOMORROW I WILL FOCUS ON . . .

HOW I'M FEELING RIGHT NOW:

 TODAY I'M NOT DRINKING BECAUSE . . .

I'M GRATEFUL FOR . . .

1.

2.

3.

> Do your homework by learning what you're
> really putting into your body. Still thirsty?

 I PRACTICED SELF-CARE BY . . .

1.

2.

3.

TODAY I ACCOMPLISHED . . .

TOMORROW I WILL FOCUS ON . . .

☀ HOW I'M FEELING RIGHT NOW:

☀ TODAY I'M NOT DRINKING BECAUSE . . .

☀ I'M GRATEFUL FOR . . .

1.

2.

3.

> Mindset matters. Sobriety is not a punishment but an act of radical self-care.

☽ I PRACTICED SELF-CARE BY . . .

1.

2.

3.

☽ TODAY I ACCOMPLISHED . . .

☽ TOMORROW I WILL FOCUS ON . . .

_____ / _____ / _____   _____ DAYS SOBER

 HOW I'M FEELING RIGHT NOW:

 TODAY I'M NOT DRINKING BECAUSE . . .

 I'M GRATEFUL FOR . . .

1.

2.

3.

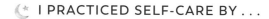
Still setting rules—only on weekends, never alone, no hard stuff? Just do the thing already! What if it all works out?

 I PRACTICED SELF-CARE BY . . .

1.

2.

3.

 TODAY I ACCOMPLISHED . . .

 TOMORROW I WILL FOCUS ON . . .

FIND YOUR
PLACE OF PEACE

Certain places can present challenges to sticking with a sobriety plan. Think about how acceptable 8:00 a.m. drinking at airports seems to be! But a little prep can help keep your focus where you want it to be. One option at the airport: bring a new fiction or quit lit book to immerse yourself in. Where will you go this week that could be a drinking trigger, and how can you find peace in those spaces?

DANGER ZONE

SACRED SPACE

 HOW I'M FEELING RIGHT NOW:

 TODAY I'M NOT DRINKING BECAUSE . . .

 I'M GRATEFUL FOR . . .

1.

2.

3.

> Stock up on nonalcoholic beverages. Have them accessible
> and ready to swap during your "witching hour."

 I PRACTICED SELF-CARE BY . . .

1.

2.

3.

 TODAY I ACCOMPLISHED . . .

 TOMORROW I WILL FOCUS ON . . .

☀ HOW I'M FEELING RIGHT NOW:

☀ TODAY I'M NOT DRINKING BECAUSE . . .

☀ I'M GRATEFUL FOR . . .

1.

2.

3.

> Refuse to allow fear and stigma to stop you
> on your journey as a nondrinker.

☾ I PRACTICED SELF-CARE BY . . .

1.

2.

3.

☾ TODAY I ACCOMPLISHED . . .

☾ TOMORROW I WILL FOCUS ON . . .

 _____ / _____ / _____   _____ **DAYS SOBER**

 HOW I'M FEELING RIGHT NOW:

 TODAY I'M NOT DRINKING BECAUSE . . .

 I'M GRATEFUL FOR . . .

1.

2.

3.

> With every drink refusal, you will gain the confidence to be open about your alcohol-free choice.

 I PRACTICED SELF-CARE BY . . .

1.

2.

3.

 TODAY I ACCOMPLISHED . . .

 TOMORROW I WILL FOCUS ON . . .

☀ HOW I'M FEELING RIGHT NOW:

😄 🙂 😐 😢 🙁 😴 😍 😕 😑 😖 🙂

☀ TODAY I'M NOT DRINKING BECAUSE . . .

☀ I'M GRATEFUL FOR . . .

1.

2.

3.

> Get inspired by downloading one podcast
> and getting one book on sobriety.

☾ I PRACTICED SELF-CARE BY . . .

1.

2.

3.

☾ TODAY I ACCOMPLISHED . . .

☾ TOMORROW I WILL FOCUS ON . . .

 DAYS SOBER

_____ / _____ / _____   _____ DAYS SOBER

 HOW I'M FEELING RIGHT NOW:

 TODAY I'M NOT DRINKING BECAUSE . . .

 I'M GRATEFUL FOR . . .

1.

2.

3.

> There's no perfect way to explore an alcohol-free life.
> Find what works best for you.

 I PRACTICED SELF-CARE BY . . .

1.

2.

3.

 TODAY I ACCOMPLISHED . . .

 TOMORROW I WILL FOCUS ON . . .

HOW I'M FEELING RIGHT NOW:

😁 🙂 😐 🙁 😕 😌 😍 😑 😣 😖 🙂

 TODAY I'M NOT DRINKING BECAUSE . . .

 I'M GRATEFUL FOR . . .

1.

2.

3.

> Your choices can be cycle breaking,
> changing the future for generations to come.

☾ I PRACTICED SELF-CARE BY . . .

1.

2.

3.

☾ TODAY I ACCOMPLISHED . . .

☾ TOMORROW I WILL FOCUS ON . . .

HAVE THE CONVERSATION

Don't be afraid or ashamed to let people know you're not drinking anymore! Keeping your sobriety a secret restricts support and accountability. And conversations can save lives. Think of all the people in your life who will benefit from your sobriety and possibly follow your lead. Make a list of the people you need to bring up to date. Determine order by who needs to hear it the most urgently or by who you'll feel most comfortable approaching first.

- _____
- _____
- _____
- _____
- _____
- _____
- _____

HOW I'M FEELING RIGHT NOW:

😊 🙂 😐 😔 🙁 😴 😍 😕 😠 😬 🙂

 TODAY I'M NOT DRINKING BECAUSE . . .

 I'M GRATEFUL FOR . . .

1.

2.

3.

> When someone doesn't respect your sobriety, run!

 I PRACTICED SELF-CARE BY . . .

1.

2.

3.

 TODAY I ACCOMPLISHED . . .

 TOMORROW I WILL FOCUS ON . . .

 HOW I'M FEELING RIGHT NOW:

 TODAY I'M NOT DRINKING BECAUSE . . .

 I'M GRATEFUL FOR . . .

1.

2.

3.

> Your worth is not determined by the
> amount of alcohol you can consume.

 I PRACTICED SELF-CARE BY . . .

1.

2.

3.

 TODAY I ACCOMPLISHED . . .

 TOMORROW I WILL FOCUS ON . . .

☀ HOW I'M FEELING RIGHT NOW:

☀ TODAY I'M NOT DRINKING BECAUSE . . .

☀ I'M GRATEFUL FOR . . .

1.

2.

3.

> You're meant for greatness. Take up space.
> Be loud. And advocate for yourself.

☾ I PRACTICED SELF-CARE BY . . .

1.

2.

3.

☾ TODAY I ACCOMPLISHED . . .

☾ TOMORROW I WILL FOCUS ON . . .

☀ HOW I'M FEELING RIGHT NOW:

☀ TODAY I'M NOT DRINKING BECAUSE . . .

☀ I'M GRATEFUL FOR . . .

  1.

  2.

  3.

>> It's important to talk and write about all of our
real feelings, instead of silencing the negative ones. <<

☾ I PRACTICED SELF-CARE BY . . .

  1.

  2.

  3.

☾ TODAY I ACCOMPLISHED . . .

☾ TOMORROW I WILL FOCUS ON . . .

HOW I'M FEELING RIGHT NOW:

 TODAY I'M NOT DRINKING BECAUSE . . .

 I'M GRATEFUL FOR . . .

   1.

   2.

   3.

> Don't fear change.
> Fear remaining in the same unhappy place.

 I PRACTICED SELF-CARE BY . . .

   1.

   2.

   3.

 TODAY I ACCOMPLISHED . . .

 TOMORROW I WILL FOCUS ON . . .

☀ HOW I'M FEELING RIGHT NOW:

😊 🙂 😐 😢 😟 😌 😍 😕 😠 😖 🙂

☀ TODAY I'M NOT DRINKING BECAUSE . . .

☀ I'M GRATEFUL FOR . . .

1.

2.

3.

> Give yourself the opportunity to
> receive all the gifts of a sober life.

 I PRACTICED SELF-CARE BY . . .

1.

2.

3.

 TODAY I ACCOMPLISHED . . .

 TOMORROW I WILL FOCUS ON . . .

DELAY AND DISTRACT

When a craving hits, be ready to meet it head-on. Your best weapon: finding a way to delay and distract for about 20 minutes—the time it takes a typical craving to pass. Add your distraction tactics to the list below:

- Listen to a podcast.
- Take a brisk walk.
- Call a friend.
- Have a dance party in your house.
- _____
- _____
- _____
- _____
- _____

☀ HOW I'M FEELING RIGHT NOW:

☀ TODAY I'M NOT DRINKING BECAUSE . . .

☀ I'M GRATEFUL FOR . . .

    1.

    2.

    3.

>>> Today's a new day. Don't give up. <<<

☾ I PRACTICED SELF-CARE BY . . .

    1.

    2.

    3.

☾ TODAY I ACCOMPLISHED . . .

☾ TOMORROW I WILL FOCUS ON . . .

HOW I'M FEELING RIGHT NOW:

 TODAY I'M NOT DRINKING BECAUSE . . .

 I'M GRATEFUL FOR . . .

1.

2.

3.

>>> If sobriety labels are holding you back, ditch them.
You don't need to define your decision. <<<

 I PRACTICED SELF-CARE BY . . .

1.

2.

3.

I TODAY I ACCOMPLISHED . . .

TOMORROW I WILL FOCUS ON . . .

 HOW I'M FEELING RIGHT NOW:

TODAY I'M NOT DRINKING BECAUSE . . .

I'M GRATEFUL FOR . . .

1.

2.

3.

> If the idea of forever is scary, think of one day at a time, building confidence and momentum.

 I PRACTICED SELF-CARE BY . . .

1.

2.

3.

TODAY I ACCOMPLISHED . . .

TOMORROW I WILL FOCUS ON . . .

HOW I'M FEELING RIGHT NOW:

 TODAY I'M NOT DRINKING BECAUSE . . .

 I'M GRATEFUL FOR . . .

    1.

    2.

    3.

 You deserve credit for each drink you pass up and every boundary you set

 I PRACTICED SELF-CARE BY . . .

    1.

    2.

    3.

 TODAY I ACCOMPLISHED . . .

 TOMORROW I WILL FOCUS ON . . .

_____ / _____ / _____   _____ DAYS SOBER

 HOW I'M FEELING RIGHT NOW:

 TODAY I'M NOT DRINKING BECAUSE . . .

 I'M GRATEFUL FOR . . .

   1.

   2.

   3.

>>> Maybe this year was never about starting
something new but putting an end to something old. <<<

 I PRACTICED SELF-CARE BY . . .

   1.

   2.

   3.

 TODAY I ACCOMPLISHED . . .

 TOMORROW I WILL FOCUS ON . . .

 HOW I'M FEELING RIGHT NOW:

TODAY I'M NOT DRINKING BECAUSE . . .

I'M GRATEFUL FOR . . .

1.

2.

3.

Get any sober support you need: journal, find a therapist, confide in a close friend, and pray or meditate.

 I PRACTICED SELF-CARE BY . . .

1.

2.

3.

TODAY I ACCOMPLISHED . . .

TOMORROW I WILL FOCUS ON . . .

MAKE SOBRIETY SWEET

When you first stop drinking, your dopamine pathways may go a bit haywire. Your brain may look for happiness in a sugar rush. Be gentle with yourself and make the best decisions possible to curb your sweet cravings. Try Cotton Candy grapes (delicious frozen) or dark chocolate chips stuffed in raspberries. List a few sweet but smart options to keep on hand.

- _____
- _____
- _____
- _____
- _____
- _____
- _____

☀ HOW I'M FEELING RIGHT NOW:

😄 🙂 😐 😕 😣 😌 😍 😶 😠 😖 🙂

☀ TODAY I'M NOT DRINKING BECAUSE . . .

☀ I'M GRATEFUL FOR . . .

1.

2.

3.

 Sobriety doesn't suck, but some people's attitudes and stereotypes about it do.

☾ I PRACTICED SELF-CARE BY . . .

1.

2.

3.

☾ TODAY I ACCOMPLISHED . . .

☾ TOMORROW I WILL FOCUS ON . . .

HOW I'M FEELING RIGHT NOW:

 TODAY I'M NOT DRINKING BECAUSE . . .

I'M GRATEFUL FOR . . .

1.

2.

3.

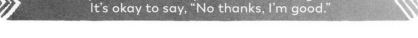

Peer pressure can keep us from declining a drink.
It's okay to say, "No thanks, I'm good."

I PRACTICED SELF-CARE BY . . .

1.

2.

3.

TODAY I ACCOMPLISHED . . .

TOMORROW I WILL FOCUS ON . . .

_____ / _____ / _____ _____ **DAYS SOBER**

☀ HOW I'M FEELING RIGHT NOW:

☀ TODAY I'M NOT DRINKING BECAUSE . . .

☀ I'M GRATEFUL FOR . . .

1.

2.

3.

> Box up the boozy decor in your home
> and reset your intentions.

 I PRACTICED SELF-CARE BY . . .

1.

2.

3.

☾ TODAY I ACCOMPLISHED . . .

☾ TOMORROW I WILL FOCUS ON . . .

☀ HOW I'M FEELING RIGHT NOW:

☀ TODAY I'M NOT DRINKING BECAUSE . . .

☀ I'M GRATEFUL FOR . . .

1.

2.

3.

You're always in the driver's seat. You get to decide what type of relationship you have with alcohol.

☾ I PRACTICED SELF-CARE BY . . .

1.

2.

3.

☾ TODAY I ACCOMPLISHED . . .

☾ TOMORROW I WILL FOCUS ON . . .

_____ / _____ / _____   _____ DAYS SOBER

 HOW I'M FEELING RIGHT NOW:

😊 🙂 😐 🙁 😟 😴 😍 😐 😠 😬 🙂

 TODAY I'M NOT DRINKING BECAUSE . . .

 I'M GRATEFUL FOR . . .

1.

2.

3.

> Even if you aren't loud about your sobriety yet, be proud.

 I PRACTICED SELF-CARE BY . . .

1.

2.

3.

 TODAY I ACCOMPLISHED . . .

 TOMORROW I WILL FOCUS ON . . .

___ / ___ / _____   _____ DAYS SOBER

☀ HOW I'M FEELING RIGHT NOW:

😄 🙂 😐 😢 😟 😴 😍 😐 😟 😖 🙂

☀ TODAY I'M NOT DRINKING BECAUSE . . .

☀ I'M GRATEFUL FOR . . .

1.

2.

3.

> The relief and solutions you're after
> will never be at the bottom of a bottle.

☾ I PRACTICED SELF-CARE BY . . .

1.

2.

3.

☾ TODAY I ACCOMPLISHED . . .

☾ TOMORROW I WILL FOCUS ON . . .

CONFIDENCE WITHOUT ALCOHOL

Drinking alcohol reduces your inhibitions while increasing dopamine, causing you to feel a burst of "liquid confidence." It's a fleeting effect that can leave you feeling deflated once the alcohol wears off. So, how do you find true confidence?

- Focus on positive self-talk.
- Practice socializing without alcohol.
- Step out of your comfort zone.
- Practice self-care habits.
- Remember: Others' opinions of you don't matter.
- _____
- _____
- _____
- _____

Add any healthful confidence boosters you can use.

☀ HOW I'M FEELING RIGHT NOW:

😀 🙂 😐 🥲 😕 😌 😍 😬 😠 😖 🙂

☀ TODAY I'M NOT DRINKING BECAUSE . . .

☀ I'M GRATEFUL FOR . . .

1.

2.

3.

> Nothing that happens today requires a drink.

☾ I PRACTICED SELF-CARE BY . . .

1.

2.

3.

☾ TODAY I ACCOMPLISHED . . .

☾ TOMORROW I WILL FOCUS ON . . .

_____ / _____ / _____　　　　　　_____ DAYS SOBER

☀ HOW I'M FEELING RIGHT NOW:

😄 🙂 😐 😢 🙁 😴 😍 😶 😑 😖 🙂

☀ TODAY I'M NOT DRINKING BECAUSE . . .

☀ I'M GRATEFUL FOR . . .

　　1.

　　2.

　　3.

 Don't think about what you've given up;
think about all that you have gained.

☾ I PRACTICED SELF-CARE BY . . .

　　1.

　　2.

　　3.

☾ TODAY I ACCOMPLISHED . . .

☾ TOMORROW I WILL FOCUS ON . . .

_____ / _____ / _____   _____ DAYS SOBER

☀ HOW I'M FEELING RIGHT NOW:

😃 🙂 😐 🙁 ☹️ 😌ᶻ 😍 😬 😠 🤢 🙂

☀ TODAY I'M NOT DRINKING BECAUSE . . .

☀ I'M GRATEFUL FOR . . .

    1.

    2.

    3.

>>> If we're kind to our bodies, they will be kind to us. <<<

☾ I PRACTICED SELF-CARE BY . . .

    1.

    2.

    3.

☾ TODAY I ACCOMPLISHED . . .

☾ TOMORROW I WILL FOCUS ON . . .

HOW I'M FEELING RIGHT NOW:

😄 🙂 😐 🙁 😟 😌 😍 😕 😠 😣 🙂

 TODAY I'M NOT DRINKING BECAUSE . . .

 I'M GRATEFUL FOR . . .

1.

2.

3.

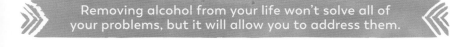
Removing alcohol from your life won't solve all of
your problems, but it will allow you to address them.

 I PRACTICED SELF-CARE BY . . .

1.

2.

3.

🌙 TODAY I ACCOMPLISHED . . .

🌙 TOMORROW I WILL FOCUS ON . . .

☀ HOW I'M FEELING RIGHT NOW:

☀ TODAY I'M NOT DRINKING BECAUSE . . .

☀ I'M GRATEFUL FOR . . .

   1.

   2.

   3.

> Challenge the drinking culture—from team-building happy hour to shots before the wedding ceremony.

☾ I PRACTICED SELF-CARE BY . . .

   1.

   2.

   3.

☾ TODAY I ACCOMPLISHED . . .

☾ TOMORROW I WILL FOCUS ON . . .

⁂ HOW I'M FEELING RIGHT NOW:

⁂ TODAY I'M NOT DRINKING BECAUSE . . .

⁂ I'M GRATEFUL FOR . . .

1.

2.

3.

> You deserve to take care of yourself,
> get healthy, and flourish.

☾ I PRACTICED SELF-CARE BY . . .

1.

2.

3.

☾ TODAY I ACCOMPLISHED . . .

☾ TOMORROW I WILL FOCUS ON . . .

YOU CAN OUTGROW . . .

- Keeping score of your past mistakes.
- Reaching for mind-altering chemicals to feel better.
- Needing to be liked by everyone.
- Speaking poorly to yourself.
- Looking outside yourself for happiness.
- Returning to a substance because next time will be different.

- _____
- _____
- _____
- _____
- _____
- _____

Add any reminders you need to hear.

_____ / _____ / _____   _____ DAYS SOBER

 HOW I'M FEELING RIGHT NOW:

TODAY I'M NOT DRINKING BECAUSE . . .

I'M GRATEFUL FOR . . .

  1.

  2.

  3.

> Peer pressure to drink is basically adult bullying.
> If you don't feel comfortable with a situation, leave.

I PRACTICED SELF-CARE BY . . .

  1.

  2.

  3.

TODAY I ACCOMPLISHED . . .

TOMORROW I WILL FOCUS ON . . .

☀ HOW I'M FEELING RIGHT NOW:

☀ TODAY I'M NOT DRINKING BECAUSE . . .

☀ I'M GRATEFUL FOR . . .

1.

2.

3.

 Hate, shame, and judgment have no place here.

☾ I PRACTICED SELF-CARE BY . . .

1.

2.

3.

☾ TODAY I ACCOMPLISHED . . .

☾ TOMORROW I WILL FOCUS ON . . .

☀ HOW I'M FEELING RIGHT NOW:

😁 🙂 😐 🙁 😕 😴 😍 😶 😠 😖 🙂

☀ TODAY I'M NOT DRINKING BECAUSE . . .

☀ I'M GRATEFUL FOR . . .

1.

2.

3.

> Being alcohol-free isn't just for a "dry" month if you don't want it to be. The benefits can last so much longer!

☾ I PRACTICED SELF-CARE BY . . .

1.

2.

3.

☾ TODAY I ACCOMPLISHED . . .

☾ TOMORROW I WILL FOCUS ON . . .

☀ HOW I'M FEELING RIGHT NOW:

😃 🙂 😐 😔 🙁 😴 😍 😕 😑 😖 🙂

☀ TODAY I'M NOT DRINKING BECAUSE . . .

☀ I'M GRATEFUL FOR . . .

1.

2.

3.

> Forgiveness, self-awareness, and
> self-compassion will set you free.

🌙 I PRACTICED SELF-CARE BY . . .

1.

2.

3.

🌙 TODAY I ACCOMPLISHED . . .

🌙 TOMORROW I WILL FOCUS ON . . .

_____ / _____ / _____   _____ DAYS SOBER

|||||||||||||||||||||||||||||||||||||||||||||||||||||||||||||||||||||||||||||||||||||||||||||||||||||||||||||||||||||

☀ HOW I'M FEELING RIGHT NOW:

😁 🙂 😐 😢 😕 😴 😍 😶 😣 😖 😋

☀ TODAY I'M NOT DRINKING BECAUSE . . .

☀ I'M GRATEFUL FOR . . .

1.

2.

3.

>>> Remove the drinking goggles. The eyes of a sober
person are filled with clarity, health, and confidence. <<<

☾ I PRACTICED SELF-CARE BY . . .

1.

2.

3.

☾ TODAY I ACCOMPLISHED . . .

☾ TOMORROW I WILL FOCUS ON . . .

HOW I'M FEELING RIGHT NOW:

TODAY I'M NOT DRINKING BECAUSE . . .

I'M GRATEFUL FOR . . .

1.

2.

3.

> The peer pressure is real. The jokes feel like jabs.
> Remain focused on the bigger picture.

 I PRACTICED SELF-CARE BY . . .

1.

2.

3.

TODAY I ACCOMPLISHED . . .

TOMORROW I WILL FOCUS ON . . .

RECLAIM YOUR JOY

The artificial high that alcohol brings is not real pleasure. Over time, it can become difficult to find joy in nonalcohol-related ways. The progression is often so minimal that we overlook or defend our drinking habits. Remind yourself what true joy can be by listing healthier sources of happiness in your life.

- _____
- _____
- _____
- _____
- _____
- _____
- _____

_____ / _____ / _____   _____ DAYS SOBER

 HOW I'M FEELING RIGHT NOW:

 TODAY I'M NOT DRINKING BECAUSE . . .

I'M GRATEFUL FOR . . .

   1.

   2.

   3.

> Align yourself with people who support you,
> cheer you on, and will love you through the journey.

 I PRACTICED SELF-CARE BY . . .

   1.

   2.

   3.

TODAY I ACCOMPLISHED . . .

TOMORROW I WILL FOCUS ON . . .

☀ HOW I'M FEELING RIGHT NOW:

😄 🙂 😐 😔 ☹️ 😴 😍 😏 😑 😖 🙂

☀ TODAY I'M NOT DRINKING BECAUSE . . .

☀ I'M GRATEFUL FOR . . .

1.

2.

3.

> You get to decide what's best for you.
> Stop the stories, excuses, and self-doubt.

☾ I PRACTICED SELF-CARE BY . . .

1.

2.

3.

☾ TODAY I ACCOMPLISHED . . .

☾ TOMORROW I WILL FOCUS ON . . .

☀ HOW I'M FEELING RIGHT NOW:

☀ TODAY I'M NOT DRINKING BECAUSE . . .

☀ I'M GRATEFUL FOR . . .

1.

2.

3.

> Be that broken record as many times
> as it takes. "Yep, still not drinking!"

☾ I PRACTICED SELF-CARE BY . . .

1.

2.

3.

☾ TODAY I ACCOMPLISHED . . .

☾ TOMORROW I WILL FOCUS ON . . .

☀ HOW I'M FEELING RIGHT NOW:

☀ TODAY I'M NOT DRINKING BECAUSE . . .

☀ I'M GRATEFUL FOR . . .

    1.

    2.

    3.

 No amount of alcohol is "good" for your health.

☽ I PRACTICED SELF-CARE BY . . .

    1.

    2.

    3.

☽ TODAY I ACCOMPLISHED . . .

☽ TOMORROW I WILL FOCUS ON . . .

☀ HOW I'M FEELING RIGHT NOW:

☀ TODAY I'M NOT DRINKING BECAUSE . . .

☀ I'M GRATEFUL FOR . . .

1.

2.

3.

> People will talk regardless. Be "that girl" who doesn't drink. Give them something inspiring to talk about.

☾ I PRACTICED SELF-CARE BY . . .

1.

2.

3.

☾ TODAY I ACCOMPLISHED . . .

☾ TOMORROW I WILL FOCUS ON . . .

☀ HOW I'M FEELING RIGHT NOW:

☀ TODAY I'M NOT DRINKING BECAUSE . . .

☀ I'M GRATEFUL FOR . . .

1.

2.

3.

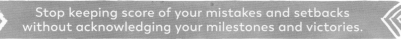

Stop keeping score of your mistakes and setbacks
without acknowledging your milestones and victories.

☾ I PRACTICED SELF-CARE BY . . .

1.

2.

3.

☾ TODAY I ACCOMPLISHED . . .

☾ TOMORROW I WILL FOCUS ON . . .

NEVER APOLOGIZE FOR . . .

- Being a powerful woman.
- Having powerful emotions.
- The shape of your body.
- Not settling.
- Choosing an alcohol-free life.
- Your success.

- _____
- _____
- _____
- _____
- _____
- _____
- _____

Add any reminders you need to hear.

☀ HOW I'M FEELING RIGHT NOW:

☀ TODAY I'M NOT DRINKING BECAUSE . . .

☀ I'M GRATEFUL FOR . . .

1.

2.

3.

> Stand strong and proud in the decisions you
> make for yourself and for your body.

☾ I PRACTICED SELF-CARE BY . . .

1.

2.

3.

☾ TODAY I ACCOMPLISHED . . .

☾ TOMORROW I WILL FOCUS ON . . .

☀ HOW I'M FEELING RIGHT NOW:

😀 🙂 😐 🙁 ☹ 😌 😍 😕 😑 😖 🙂

☀ TODAY I'M NOT DRINKING BECAUSE . . .

☀ I'M GRATEFUL FOR . . .

1.

2.

3.

Just like dairy, cigarettes, meat, or sugar, if you don't like the way alcohol makes you feel, cut it out.

☾ I PRACTICED SELF-CARE BY . . .

1.

2.

3.

☾ TODAY I ACCOMPLISHED . . .

☾ TOMORROW I WILL FOCUS ON . . .

_____ / _____ / _____   _____ DAYS SOBER

☀ HOW I'M FEELING RIGHT NOW:

😄 🙂 😐 🙁 😟 😌ᶻ 😍 😑 😠 😖 🙂

☀ TODAY I'M NOT DRINKING BECAUSE . . .

☀ I'M GRATEFUL FOR . . .

1.

2.

3.

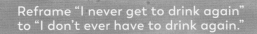
Reframe "I never get to drink again"
to "I don't ever have to drink again."

☾ I PRACTICED SELF-CARE BY . . .

1.

2.

3.

☾ TODAY I ACCOMPLISHED . . .

☾ TOMORROW I WILL FOCUS ON . . .

_____ / _____ / _____   _____ DAYS SOBER

 HOW I'M FEELING RIGHT NOW:

 TODAY I'M NOT DRINKING BECAUSE . . .

I'M GRATEFUL FOR . . .

1.

2.

3.

>>> Sometimes we find our path when we least expect it. <<<

I PRACTICED SELF-CARE BY . . .

1.

2.

3.

TODAY I ACCOMPLISHED . . .

TOMORROW I WILL FOCUS ON . . .

☀ HOW I'M FEELING RIGHT NOW:

☀ TODAY I'M NOT DRINKING BECAUSE . . .

☀ I'M GRATEFUL FOR . . .

1.

2.

3.

Self-care is community care. Everyone around you benefits from your healing and well-being.

☾ I PRACTICED SELF-CARE BY . . .

1.

2.

3.

☾ TODAY I ACCOMPLISHED . . .

☾ TOMORROW I WILL FOCUS ON . . .

 HOW I'M FEELING RIGHT NOW:

 TODAY I'M NOT DRINKING BECAUSE . . .

 I'M GRATEFUL FOR . . .

1.

2.

3.

> Alcohol is the most abused anxiety drug—
> and it doesn't work.

 I PRACTICED SELF-CARE BY . . .

1.

2.

3.

 TODAY I ACCOMPLISHED . . .

 TOMORROW I WILL FOCUS ON . . .

QUESTIONING IF YOU'RE READY?

If you're not happy with or even just unsure about your relationship with alcohol, that's all you need to know. You're ready enough right now. Ask yourself questions like:

WHY DO/DID I DRINK?

_____

WHAT DO I BELIEVE TO BE TRUE ABOUT ALCOHOL?

_____

HOW DOES ALCOHOL _REALLY_ MAKE ME FEEL?

_____

WHAT IS IT GOING TO COST ME IF I DON'T TAKE A BREAK?

_____

☀ HOW I'M FEELING RIGHT NOW:

☀ TODAY I'M NOT DRINKING BECAUSE . . .

☀ I'M GRATEFUL FOR . . .

1.

2.

3.

> It's an incredible feeling to make a decision
> and end the tug-of-war inside your mind.

 I PRACTICED SELF-CARE BY . . .

1.

2.

3.

 TODAY I ACCOMPLISHED . . .

☾ TOMORROW I WILL FOCUS ON . . .

_____ / _____ / _____   _____ DAYS SOBER

 HOW I'M FEELING RIGHT NOW:

😀 🙂 😐 😓 😕 😴 😍 😶 😣 😖 🙂

 TODAY I'M NOT DRINKING BECAUSE . . .

 I'M GRATEFUL FOR . . .

1.

2.

3.

> Alcohol does not need to be an accessory
> for adulthood or motherhood.

 I PRACTICED SELF-CARE BY . . .

1.

2.

3.

 TODAY I ACCOMPLISHED . . .

 TOMORROW I WILL FOCUS ON . . .

HOW I'M FEELING RIGHT NOW:

TODAY I'M NOT DRINKING BECAUSE . . .

I'M GRATEFUL FOR . . .

1.

2.

3.

> You just might find that giving up alcohol is the best thing you've ever done for your mental health.

 I PRACTICED SELF-CARE BY . . .

1.

2.

3.

TODAY I ACCOMPLISHED . . .

TOMORROW I WILL FOCUS ON . . .

_____ / _____ / _____   _____ DAYS SOBER

 HOW I'M FEELING RIGHT NOW:

😄 🙂 😐 🙁 😟 😴 😍 😐 😠 😖 🙂

✳ TODAY I'M NOT DRINKING BECAUSE . . .

✳ I'M GRATEFUL FOR . . .

    1.

    2.

    3.

>>> You're not alone in sobriety:
one-third of the population doesn't drink alcohol. <<<

☾ I PRACTICED SELF-CARE BY . . .

    1.

    2.

    3.

☾ TODAY I ACCOMPLISHED . . .

☾ TOMORROW I WILL FOCUS ON . . .

 HOW I'M FEELING RIGHT NOW:

 TODAY I'M NOT DRINKING BECAUSE . . .

 I'M GRATEFUL FOR . . .

1.

2.

3.

We can change the culture by offering sophisticated alcohol-free alternatives for any alcohol-fueled celebrations.

I PRACTICED SELF-CARE BY . . .

1.

2.

3.

TODAY I ACCOMPLISHED . . .

TOMORROW I WILL FOCUS ON . . .

☀ HOW I'M FEELING RIGHT NOW:

😁 🙂 😐 🙁 😕 😌ᶻ 😍 😶 😠 😵 🙂

☀ TODAY I'M NOT DRINKING BECAUSE . . .

☀ I'M GRATEFUL FOR . . .

1.

2.

3.

 Wherever you are, your zero-proof drink should be.

☾ I PRACTICED SELF-CARE BY . . .

1.

2.

3.

☾ TODAY I ACCOMPLISHED . . .

☾ TOMORROW I WILL FOCUS ON . . .

DEFEAT THE WITCHING HOUR

The urge to drink often hits between late afternoon and evening. To stay sane and sober:

- Avoid the commute by your local bar or gas station.
- Meet nondrinking friends for dinner or a movie.
- Stock up on zero-proof alternatives to grab and enjoy.
- Stay busy. Check the mail, listen to a podcast, or attend a virtual support meeting.
- Reach out to someone who understands why it's important that you stick to your decision not to drink and who can help you stay accountable.

- _____

- _____

- _____

- _____

Add any other tactics that could work for you.

☀ HOW I'M FEELING RIGHT NOW:

😄 🙂 😐 🙁 ☹️ 😴 😍 😕 😑 😖 🙂

☀ TODAY I'M NOT DRINKING BECAUSE . . .

☀ I'M GRATEFUL FOR . . .

1.

2.

3.

Take a moment to see you living your best life.

 I PRACTICED SELF-CARE BY . . .

1.

2.

3.

 TODAY I ACCOMPLISHED . . .

☾ TOMORROW I WILL FOCUS ON . . .

HOW I'M FEELING RIGHT NOW:

 TODAY I'M NOT DRINKING BECAUSE . . .

 I'M GRATEFUL FOR . . .

1.

2.

3.

Clear your physical and social spaces of triggers—from "five o'clock somewhere" T-shirts to "wine mom" memes.

 I PRACTICED SELF-CARE BY . . .

1.

2.

3.

 TODAY I ACCOMPLISHED . . .

 TOMORROW I WILL FOCUS ON . . .

HOW I'M FEELING RIGHT NOW:

😄 🙂 😐 🙁 😕 😌ᶻ 😍 😐 😬 😵 🙂

 TODAY I'M NOT DRINKING BECAUSE . . .

 I'M GRATEFUL FOR . . .

   1.

   2.

   3.

>>> If no one's told you today, you're doing an amazing job. <<<

I PRACTICED SELF-CARE BY . . .

   1.

   2.

   3.

TODAY I ACCOMPLISHED . . .

TOMORROW I WILL FOCUS ON . . .

_____ / _____ / _____   _____ DAYS SOBER

 HOW I'M FEELING RIGHT NOW:

 TODAY I'M NOT DRINKING BECAUSE . . .

 I'M GRATEFUL FOR . . .

   1.

   2.

   3.

Do more of what makes you truly happy,
not "alcohol happy."

 I PRACTICED SELF-CARE BY . . .

   1.

   2.

   3.

 TODAY I ACCOMPLISHED . . .

 TOMORROW I WILL FOCUS ON . . .

☀ HOW I'M FEELING RIGHT NOW:

😄 🙂 😐 😔 😕 😴 😍 😑 😠 😰 🙂

☀ TODAY I'M NOT DRINKING BECAUSE . . .

☀ I'M GRATEFUL FOR . . .

1.

2.

3.

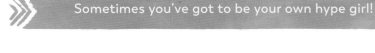

Sometimes you've got to be your own hype girl!

☾ I PRACTICED SELF-CARE BY . . .

1.

2.

3.

☾ TODAY I ACCOMPLISHED . . .

☾ TOMORROW I WILL FOCUS ON . . .

 _____ / _____ / _____   _____ DAYS SOBER

 HOW I'M FEELING RIGHT NOW:

TODAY I'M NOT DRINKING BECAUSE . . .

I'M GRATEFUL FOR . . .

1.

2.

3.

 Show up for your own life and truly love it.

I PRACTICED SELF-CARE BY . . .

1.

2.

3.

TODAY I ACCOMPLISHED . . .

TOMORROW I WILL FOCUS ON . . .

STORY LINES ABOUT ALCOHOL

Ask yourself whether each statement is honestly true for you. Add any other story lines you find yourself encountering in your social life or in your head.

One glass is healthy.

I can have just one.

I'm not hurting anyone.

Alcohol eases my anxiety.

_____ / _____ / _____   _____ DAYS SOBER

☀ HOW I'M FEELING RIGHT NOW:

😀 🙂 😐 😢 ☹ 😴 😍 😐 😣 😖 🙂

☀ TODAY I'M NOT DRINKING BECAUSE . . .

☀ I'M GRATEFUL FOR . . .

1.

2.

3.

> Everything you need is already inside of you: the grit, determination, permission, answers, and power.

☾ I PRACTICED SELF-CARE BY . . .

1.

2.

3.

☾ TODAY I ACCOMPLISHED . . .

☾ TOMORROW I WILL FOCUS ON . . .

_____ / _____ / _____   _____ DAYS SOBER

☀ HOW I'M FEELING RIGHT NOW:

☀ TODAY I'M NOT DRINKING BECAUSE . . .

☀ I'M GRATEFUL FOR . . .

1.

2.

3.

>>> Not everyone who says "no thanks" is an alcoholic. <<<

☾ I PRACTICED SELF-CARE BY . . .

1.

2.

3.

☾ TODAY I ACCOMPLISHED . . .

☾ TOMORROW I WILL FOCUS ON . . .

HOW I'M FEELING RIGHT NOW:

 TODAY I'M NOT DRINKING BECAUSE . . .

 I'M GRATEFUL FOR . . .

1.

2.

3.

> Success and failure are on the same road.
> Success is just further down the road.

 I PRACTICED SELF-CARE BY . . .

1.

2.

3.

 TODAY I ACCOMPLISHED . . .

 TOMORROW I WILL FOCUS ON . . .

☀ HOW I'M FEELING RIGHT NOW:

😀 🙂 😐 😢 😕 😴 😍 😑 😠 😖 🙂

☀ TODAY I'M NOT DRINKING BECAUSE . . .

☀ I'M GRATEFUL FOR . . .

1.

2.

3.

> Not every unpopular choice is a mistake,
> but not every popular choice is beneficial either.

☾ I PRACTICED SELF-CARE BY . . .

1.

2.

3.

☾ TODAY I ACCOMPLISHED . . .

☾ TOMORROW I WILL FOCUS ON . . .

HOW I'M FEELING RIGHT NOW:

 TODAY I'M NOT DRINKING BECAUSE . . .

I'M GRATEFUL FOR . . .

1.

2.

3.

Truth: You don't need alcohol to grieve,
parent, celebrate, or even relax.

 I PRACTICED SELF-CARE BY . . .

1.

2.

3.

TODAY I ACCOMPLISHED . . .

TOMORROW I WILL FOCUS ON . . .

☀ HOW I'M FEELING RIGHT NOW:

☀ TODAY I'M NOT DRINKING BECAUSE . . .

☀ I'M GRATEFUL FOR . . .

1.

2.

3.

> Sometimes all it takes is believing that it's possible.

☾ I PRACTICED SELF-CARE BY . . .

1.

2.

3.

☾ TODAY I ACCOMPLISHED . . .

☾ TOMORROW I WILL FOCUS ON . . .

YOUR PHONE IS YOUR FRIEND

Your phone is an amazing asset. Think about all it offers:

- Supportive contacts, especially _____
  and _____
- Sober social media accounts
- Helpful hotlines
- Zoom meetings
- Meditation and breathing apps
- Podcasts and playlists
- Walk/run routes
- _____
- _____
- _____
- _____
- _____

Add any other ways you can turn to your phone.

_____ / _____ / _____   _____ DAYS SOBER

 HOW I'M FEELING RIGHT NOW:

☀ TODAY I'M NOT DRINKING BECAUSE . . .

☀ I'M GRATEFUL FOR . . .

1.

2.

3.

> A lot of things can "run in the family" until they run into you. It's within your power to disrupt a cycle.

☾ I PRACTICED SELF-CARE BY . . .

1.

2.

3.

☾ TODAY I ACCOMPLISHED . . .

☾ TOMORROW I WILL FOCUS ON . . .

_____ / _____ / _____   _____ DAYS SOBER

☀ HOW I'M FEELING RIGHT NOW:

😄 🙂 😐 😢 ☹ 😴 😍 😶 😠 😖 🙂

☀ TODAY I'M NOT DRINKING BECAUSE . . .

☀ I'M GRATEFUL FOR . . .

1.

2.

3.

>>> The progress you've made counts. <<<

☽ I PRACTICED SELF-CARE BY . . .

1.

2.

3.

☽ TODAY I ACCOMPLISHED . . .

☽ TOMORROW I WILL FOCUS ON . . .

_____ / _____ / _____   _____ DAYS SOBER

☀ HOW I'M FEELING RIGHT NOW:

☀ TODAY I'M NOT DRINKING BECAUSE . . .

☀ I'M GRATEFUL FOR . . .

1.

2.

3.

> Falling down is allowed; getting back up is mandatory.
> Get your butt up and keep going!

☾ I PRACTICED SELF-CARE BY . . .

1.

2.

3.

☾ TODAY I ACCOMPLISHED . . .

☾ TOMORROW I WILL FOCUS ON . . .

HOW I'M FEELING RIGHT NOW:

 TODAY I'M NOT DRINKING BECAUSE . . .

I'M GRATEFUL FOR . . .

1.

2.

3.

> Whatever you are feeling today, know that
> you are not the only one who feels this way.

 I PRACTICED SELF-CARE BY . . .

1.

2.

3.

TODAY I ACCOMPLISHED . . .

TOMORROW I WILL FOCUS ON . . .

☀ HOW I'M FEELING RIGHT NOW:

☀ TODAY I'M NOT DRINKING BECAUSE . . .

☀ I'M GRATEFUL FOR . . .

1.

2.

3.

> We can empower and encourage one another to get through
> the hard parts of life without relying on a carcinogen.

☾ I PRACTICED SELF-CARE BY . . .

1.

2.

3.

☾ TODAY I ACCOMPLISHED . . .

☾ TOMORROW I WILL FOCUS ON . . .

 HOW I'M FEELING RIGHT NOW:

 TODAY I'M NOT DRINKING BECAUSE . . .

 I'M GRATEFUL FOR . . .

    1.

    2.

    3.

> Remember that while alcohol can produce short-term stimulating effects, it is actually a depressant.

🌙 I PRACTICED SELF-CARE BY . . .

    1.

    2.

    3.

🌙 TODAY I ACCOMPLISHED . . .

🌙 TOMORROW I WILL FOCUS ON . . .

HOW I'M FEELING RIGHT NOW:

TODAY I'M NOT DRINKING BECAUSE . . .

I'M GRATEFUL FOR . . .

1.

2.

3.

> Whatever is hard for you in your life
> right now, being sober will help.

I PRACTICED SELF-CARE BY . . .

1.

2.

3.

TODAY I ACCOMPLISHED . . .

TOMORROW I WILL FOCUS ON . . .

_____ / _____ / _____    _____ DAYS SOBER

 HOW I'M FEELING RIGHT NOW:

TODAY I'M NOT DRINKING BECAUSE . . .

I'M GRATEFUL FOR . . .

   1.

   2.

   3.

> Create new habits that you feel good about
> and that align with your core values and goals.

 I PRACTICED SELF-CARE BY . . .

   1.

   2.

   3.

 TODAY I ACCOMPLISHED . . .

TOMORROW I WILL FOCUS ON . . .

ALWAYS REMEMBER . . .

- You are beautiful—inside and out.
- You are strong and capable.
- You are worthy and good enough.
- You don't have to be anyone but yourself.
- You are perfectly imperfect.
- You have passion waiting to be unleashed.
- You don't need alcohol to be accepted.

- _____
- _____
- _____
- _____
- _____
- _____

Add any reminders you need to hear.

_____ / _____ / _____   _____ DAYS SOBER

☀ HOW I'M FEELING RIGHT NOW:

😁 🙂 😐 😢 🙁 😴 😍 😕 😠 😖 🙂

☀ TODAY I'M NOT DRINKING BECAUSE . . .

☀ I'M GRATEFUL FOR . . .

1.

2.

3.

>> Your life is always speaking and guiding
you toward your next step. <<

🌙 I PRACTICED SELF-CARE BY . . .

1.

2.

3.

🌙 TODAY I ACCOMPLISHED . . .

🌙 TOMORROW I WILL FOCUS ON . . .

HOW I'M FEELING RIGHT NOW:

 TODAY I'M NOT DRINKING BECAUSE . . .

 I'M GRATEFUL FOR . . .

1.

2.

3.

> When you have a head full of sobriety,
> drinking is never the same.

 I PRACTICED SELF-CARE BY . . .

1.

2.

3.

 TODAY I ACCOMPLISHED . . .

 TOMORROW I WILL FOCUS ON . . .

☀ HOW I'M FEELING RIGHT NOW:

☀ TODAY I'M NOT DRINKING BECAUSE . . .

☀ I'M GRATEFUL FOR . . .

    1.

    2.

    3.

 Alcohol is synthetic confidence; being sober forces you to build your own confidence.

☾ I PRACTICED SELF-CARE BY . . .

    1.

    2.

    3.

☾ TODAY I ACCOMPLISHED . . .

☾ TOMORROW I WILL FOCUS ON . . .

 HOW I'M FEELING RIGHT NOW:

 TODAY I'M NOT DRINKING BECAUSE . . .

 I'M GRATEFUL FOR . . .

1.

2.

3.

> Don't allow fewer social invitations to
> detour you from your goal. Host your own fun!

 I PRACTICED SELF-CARE BY . . .

1.

2.

3.

🌙 TODAY I ACCOMPLISHED . . .

🌙 TOMORROW I WILL FOCUS ON . . .

_____ / _____ / _____   _____ DAYS SOBER

☀ HOW I'M FEELING RIGHT NOW:

😊 🙂 😐 😓 😕 😴 😍 😑 😦 😖 🙂

☀ TODAY I'M NOT DRINKING BECAUSE . . .

☀ I'M GRATEFUL FOR . . .

1.

2.

3.

> Seek things that bring you joy, friendships with substance, and a support system that keeps you accountable.

☾ I PRACTICED SELF-CARE BY . . .

1.

2.

3.

☾ TODAY I ACCOMPLISHED . . .

☾ TOMORROW I WILL FOCUS ON . . .

☀ HOW I'M FEELING RIGHT NOW:

☀ TODAY I'M NOT DRINKING BECAUSE . . .

☀ I'M GRATEFUL FOR . . .

1.

2.

3.

> Trust that you will end up where you need to be,
> even if you don't know how it's going to happen.

☾ I PRACTICED SELF-CARE BY . . .

1.

2.

3.

☾ TODAY I ACCOMPLISHED . . .

☾ TOMORROW I WILL FOCUS ON . . .

HOW I'M FEELING RIGHT NOW:

 **TODAY I'M NOT DRINKING BECAUSE . . .**

I'M GRATEFUL FOR . . .

1.

2.

3.

> There is always someone out there for you. Sometimes you have to reach out instead of waiting to be reached.

 I PRACTICED SELF-CARE BY . . .

1.

2.

3.

 TODAY I ACCOMPLISHED . . .

TOMORROW I WILL FOCUS ON . . .

_____ / _____ / _____   _____ DAYS SOBER

 HOW I'M FEELING RIGHT NOW:

😄 🙂 😐 🥺 😟 😴 😍 😶 😠 😖 🙂

 TODAY I'M NOT DRINKING BECAUSE . . .

 I'M GRATEFUL FOR . . .

1.

2.

3.

> Feel empowered and confident in making a
> healthy and responsible decision for you!

🌙 I PRACTICED SELF-CARE BY . . .

1.

2.

3.

🌙 TODAY I ACCOMPLISHED . . .

🌙 TOMORROW I WILL FOCUS ON . . .

NEW HABITS TO BUILD

Habits are small decisions you make and actions you perform every day. Essentially, what you repeatedly do forms the person you are. Over the course of your life, you'll pick up bad habits. Once you realize those habits aren't serving you, build new ones. Establishing habits that align with your values takes discipline and consistency, but it's worth it. Tailor this list of habits to you:

- Drink lots of water.
- Eat greens.
- Exercise.
- Get out in nature.
- Fill your head with positive self-talk.

- _____
- _____
- _____
- _____

_____ / _____ / _____   _____ DAYS SOBER

☀ HOW I'M FEELING RIGHT NOW:

😀 🙂 😐 🙁 😕 😌 😍 😶 😬 😖 🙂

☀ TODAY I'M NOT DRINKING BECAUSE . . .

☀ I'M GRATEFUL FOR . . .

1.

2.

3.

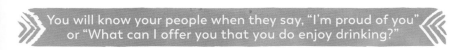

You will know your people when they say, "I'm proud of you" or "What can I offer you that you do enjoy drinking?"

☽ I PRACTICED SELF-CARE BY . . .

1.

2.

3.

☽ TODAY I ACCOMPLISHED . . .

☽ TOMORROW I WILL FOCUS ON . . .

☀ HOW I'M FEELING RIGHT NOW:

☀ TODAY I'M NOT DRINKING BECAUSE . . .

☀ I'M GRATEFUL FOR . . .

1.

2.

3.

Sobriety is better than even pumpkin spice.

☾ I PRACTICED SELF-CARE BY . . .

1.

2.

3.

☾ TODAY I ACCOMPLISHED . . .

☾ TOMORROW I WILL FOCUS ON . . .

HOW I'M FEELING RIGHT NOW:

 TODAY I'M NOT DRINKING BECAUSE . . .

 I'M GRATEFUL FOR . . .

1.

2.

3.

> Feeling down on a traditionally boozy holiday?
> Call some sober sisters and make your own party!

 I PRACTICED SELF-CARE BY . . .

1.

2.

3.

TODAY I ACCOMPLISHED . . .

TOMORROW I WILL FOCUS ON . . .

☀ HOW I'M FEELING RIGHT NOW:

😄 🙂 😐 😣 🙁 😴 😍 😬 😑 🥴 🙂

☀ TODAY I'M NOT DRINKING BECAUSE . . .

☀ I'M GRATEFUL FOR . . .

1.

2.

3.

>> Never stop reminding yourself and the people
you care about that it's okay to not drink. <<

☾ I PRACTICED SELF-CARE BY . . .

1.

2.

3.

☾ TODAY I ACCOMPLISHED . . .

☾ TOMORROW I WILL FOCUS ON . . .

☀ HOW I'M FEELING RIGHT NOW:

😃 🙂 😐 🙁 😟 😌ᶻ 😍 😐 😠 😖 🙂

☀ TODAY I'M NOT DRINKING BECAUSE . . .

☀ I'M GRATEFUL FOR . . .

1.

2.

3.

 Need motivation? The kids in our lives are watching.
We can't tell them not to drink while we're using it to cope.

☾ I PRACTICED SELF-CARE BY . . .

1.

2.

3.

☾ TODAY I ACCOMPLISHED . . .

☾ TOMORROW I WILL FOCUS ON . . .

 HOW I'M FEELING RIGHT NOW:

 TODAY I'M NOT DRINKING BECAUSE . . .

I'M GRATEFUL FOR . . .

1.

2.

3.

> Eat for energy. Sleep for balance.
> Sweat for sanity. Drink for hydration.

 I PRACTICED SELF-CARE BY . . .

1.

2.

3.

TODAY I ACCOMPLISHED . . .

TOMORROW I WILL FOCUS ON . . .

☀ HOW I'M FEELING RIGHT NOW:

😊 🙂 😐 😞 😕 😴 😍 😶 😣 😖 🙂

☀ TODAY I'M NOT DRINKING BECAUSE . . .

☀ I'M GRATEFUL FOR . . .

1.

2.

3.

 Alcohol is not the mascot for motherhood or adulthood.

☾ I PRACTICED SELF-CARE BY . . .

1.

2.

3.

☾ TODAY I ACCOMPLISHED . . .

☾ TOMORROW I WILL FOCUS ON . . .

☀ HOW I'M FEELING RIGHT NOW:

☀ TODAY I'M NOT DRINKING BECAUSE . . .

☀ I'M GRATEFUL FOR . . .

1.

2.

3.

> We can debunk the taboo around alcohol-free living and normalize sobriety as a proud choice, not a life sentence.

☾ I PRACTICED SELF-CARE BY . . .

1.

2.

3.

☾ TODAY I ACCOMPLISHED . . .

☾ TOMORROW I WILL FOCUS ON . . .

BEYOND DAY COUNTING

Don't be discouraged by a number. Day counting is not the only way to track progress on an alcohol-free journey. Putting all your eggs in one basket can be more harmful than helpful to some. Take time to reflect and come up with your own list of sober victories. A few ideas: clearer face and less bloat, kids able to drink out of your cup, money saved, remembering every minute of the wedding you attended.

- _____
- _____
- _____
- _____
- _____
- _____

☀ HOW I'M FEELING RIGHT NOW:

☀ TODAY I'M NOT DRINKING BECAUSE . . .

☀ I'M GRATEFUL FOR . . .

1.

2.

3.

> Keep showing up in sobriety and you'll be
> surprised how things begin to shift.

☾ I PRACTICED SELF-CARE BY . . .

1.

2.

3.

☾ TODAY I ACCOMPLISHED . . .

☾ TOMORROW I WILL FOCUS ON . . .

HOW I'M FEELING RIGHT NOW:

😄 🙂 😐 😢 😦 😴 😍 😑 😠 😖 🙂

 TODAY I'M NOT DRINKING BECAUSE . . .

 I'M GRATEFUL FOR . . .

   1.

   2.

   3.

> Sobriety teaches us to feel it all—the good, the bad, the messy. Without feeling, there will never be true healing.

🌙 I PRACTICED SELF-CARE BY . . .

   1.

   2.

   3.

🌙 TODAY I ACCOMPLISHED . . .

🌙 TOMORROW I WILL FOCUS ON . . .

☀ HOW I'M FEELING RIGHT NOW:

😀 🙂 😐 😔 😟 😴 😍 😑 😠 😖 🙂

☀ TODAY I'M NOT DRINKING BECAUSE . . .

☀ I'M GRATEFUL FOR . . .

1.

2.

3.

> When we're exhausted, big alcohol claims to come in and save the day. Wine is only self-care in the marketing.

☾ I PRACTICED SELF-CARE BY . . .

1.

2.

3.

☾ TODAY I ACCOMPLISHED . . .

☾ TOMORROW I WILL FOCUS ON . . .

☀ HOW I'M FEELING RIGHT NOW:

☀ TODAY I'M NOT DRINKING BECAUSE . . .

☀ I'M GRATEFUL FOR . . .

    1.

    2.

    3.

>> So many people are admiring your strength;
don't doubt yourself over the few who don't. <<

☾ I PRACTICED SELF-CARE BY . . .

    1.

    2.

    3.

☾ TODAY I ACCOMPLISHED . . .

☾ TOMORROW I WILL FOCUS ON . . .

_____ / _____ / _____   _____ DAYS SOBER

☀ HOW I'M FEELING RIGHT NOW:

☀ TODAY I'M NOT DRINKING BECAUSE . . .

 I'M GRATEFUL FOR . . .

1.

2.

3.

> Here's your permission slip to block, mute, or
> unfollow anyone who isn't aligned with your lifestyle.

☽ I PRACTICED SELF-CARE BY . . .

1.

2.

3.

☽ TODAY I ACCOMPLISHED . . .

☽ TOMORROW I WILL FOCUS ON . . .

HOW I'M FEELING RIGHT NOW:

😁 🙂 😐 🙁 😣 😴 😍 😑 😠 😖 🙂

 TODAY I'M NOT DRINKING BECAUSE . . .

 I'M GRATEFUL FOR . . .

1.

2.

3.

>>> Got 99 problems? Finding peace with
sobriety will likely solve 96 of them! <<<

🌙 **I PRACTICED SELF-CARE BY . . .**

1.

2.

3.

🌙 **TODAY I ACCOMPLISHED . . .**

🌙 **TOMORROW I WILL FOCUS ON . . .**

HOW I'M FEELING RIGHT NOW:

 TODAY I'M NOT DRINKING BECAUSE . . .

 I'M GRATEFUL FOR . . .

1.

2.

3.

> Whatever plans you have for the weekend, remember that no celebration or difficult emotions require a drink.

 I PRACTICED SELF-CARE BY . . .

1.

2.

3.

 TODAY I ACCOMPLISHED . . .

 TOMORROW I WILL FOCUS ON . . .

HOW I'M FEELING RIGHT NOW:

😀 🙂 😐 😢 🙁 😌ᶻ 😍 😶 😠 😖 🙂

 TODAY I'M NOT DRINKING BECAUSE . . .

 I'M GRATEFUL FOR . . .

    1.

    2.

    3.

>>> The longer you pretend to be someone you're not,
the more you risk forgetting who you really are. <<<

🌙 I PRACTICED SELF-CARE BY . . .

    1.

    2.

    3.

🌙 TODAY I ACCOMPLISHED . . .

🌙 TOMORROW I WILL FOCUS ON . . .

SOBER SPLURGES

Whatever the price of your favorite drink, it's costing you in other parts of your life too. Where can you shift your booze budget and get more true benefits? Travel, gym membership, massages, educational opportunities . . . ?

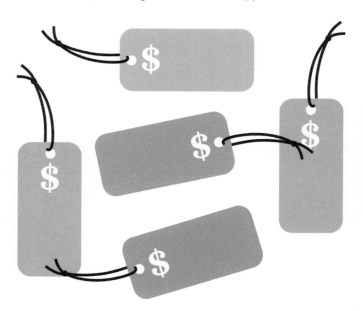

HOW I'M FEELING RIGHT NOW:

😃 🙂 😐 😔 😟 😌ᶻ 😍 😕 😣 😖 🙂

 TODAY I'M NOT DRINKING BECAUSE . . .

 I'M GRATEFUL FOR . . .

1.

2.

3.

>>> You're going to have obstacles in life, but you don't have to be one of them. Treat yourself with love. <<<

 I PRACTICED SELF-CARE BY . . .

1.

2.

3.

 TODAY I ACCOMPLISHED . . .

 TOMORROW I WILL FOCUS ON . . .

☀ HOW I'M FEELING RIGHT NOW:

☀ TODAY I'M NOT DRINKING BECAUSE . . .

☀ I'M GRATEFUL FOR . . .

   1.

   2.

   3.

Your worst day sober will always be better than your best day drunk.

☾ I PRACTICED SELF-CARE BY . . .

   1.

   2.

   3.

☾ TODAY I ACCOMPLISHED . . .

☾ TOMORROW I WILL FOCUS ON . . .

HOW I'M FEELING RIGHT NOW:

😃 🙂 😐 😔 😟 😴 😍 😕 😠 😬 🙂

 TODAY I'M NOT DRINKING BECAUSE . . .

 I'M GRATEFUL FOR . . .

1.

2.

3.

> For whatever reason you quit drinking,
> stay sober for you.

🌙 I PRACTICED SELF-CARE BY . . .

1.

2.

3.

🌙 TODAY I ACCOMPLISHED . . .

🌙 TOMORROW I WILL FOCUS ON . . .

☀ HOW I'M FEELING RIGHT NOW:

☀ TODAY I'M NOT DRINKING BECAUSE . . .

☀ I'M GRATEFUL FOR . . .

   1.

   2.

   3.

> You can detox from wine culture—
> choose the accounts and people you follow wisely.

 I PRACTICED SELF-CARE BY . . .

   1.

   2.

   3.

☾ TODAY I ACCOMPLISHED . . .

☾ TOMORROW I WILL FOCUS ON . . .

☀ HOW I'M FEELING RIGHT NOW:

☀ TODAY I'M NOT DRINKING BECAUSE . . .

☀ I'M GRATEFUL FOR . . .

1.

2.

3.

>>> You'll never wake up upset that you didn't drink. <<<

☾ I PRACTICED SELF-CARE BY . . .

1.

2.

3.

☾ TODAY I ACCOMPLISHED . . .

☾ TOMORROW I WILL FOCUS ON . . .

_____ / _____ / _____   _____ DAYS SOBER

☀ HOW I'M FEELING RIGHT NOW:

😄 🙂 😐 😥 🙁 😴 😍 😕 😣 😖 🙂

☀ TODAY I'M NOT DRINKING BECAUSE . . .

☀ I'M GRATEFUL FOR . . .

1.

2.

3.

>> Be guided by purpose over popularity.
One day, we will normalize sobriety. <<

☾ I PRACTICED SELF-CARE BY . . .

1.

2.

3.

☾ TODAY I ACCOMPLISHED . . .

☾ TOMORROW I WILL FOCUS ON . . .

HOW I'M FEELING RIGHT NOW:

😁 🙂 😐 😢 😕 😴 😍 😕 😠 😖 🙂

 TODAY I'M NOT DRINKING BECAUSE . . .

 I'M GRATEFUL FOR . . .

   1.

   2.

   3.

>>> Whether it's naysayers or self-doubt blowing negativity into your face, stand your ground and roar. <<<

🌙 I PRACTICED SELF-CARE BY . . .

   1.

   2.

   3.

🌙 TODAY I ACCOMPLISHED . . .

🌙 TOMORROW I WILL FOCUS ON . . .

_____ / _____ / _____   _____ DAYS SOBER

 HOW I'M FEELING RIGHT NOW:

😄 🙂 😐 🙁 ☹️ 😴 😍 😐 😠 😖 🙂

 TODAY I'M NOT DRINKING BECAUSE . . .

 I'M GRATEFUL FOR . . .

1.

2.

3.

> Remember that you're building something
> that won't wear off in an hour or two.

 I PRACTICED SELF-CARE BY . . .

1.

2.

3.

 TODAY I ACCOMPLISHED . . .

 TOMORROW I WILL FOCUS ON . . .

LET'S NORMALIZE . . .

- Asking for help.
- Going to therapy.
- Alcohol-free living.
- Saying no.
- Talking about mental health.
- Taking medication.
- Addiction treatment.
- Healing trauma.
- Self-care as essential—not selfish.
- _____
- _____
- _____
- _____
- _____

Add anything else that's important to you.

HOW I'M FEELING RIGHT NOW:

 TODAY I'M NOT DRINKING BECAUSE . . .

 I'M GRATEFUL FOR . . .

    1.

    2.

    3.

> Dream big—make a vision board of all the things you can and will do as you live an alcohol-free life.

 I PRACTICED SELF-CARE BY . . .

    1.

    2.

    3.

 TODAY I ACCOMPLISHED . . .

 TOMORROW I WILL FOCUS ON . . .

☀ HOW I'M FEELING RIGHT NOW:

☀ TODAY I'M NOT DRINKING BECAUSE . . .

☀ I'M GRATEFUL FOR . . .

1.

2.

3.

Remember H.A.L.T. when you're on the go.
Try to avoid getting hungry, angry, lonely, or tired.

☾ I PRACTICED SELF-CARE BY . . .

1.

2.

3.

☾ TODAY I ACCOMPLISHED . . .

☾ TOMORROW I WILL FOCUS ON . . .

_____ / _____ / _____   _____ DAYS SOBER

 HOW I'M FEELING RIGHT NOW:

😀 🙂 😐 🙁 ☹️ 😌ᶻ 😍 😕 😠 😖 🙂

 TODAY I'M NOT DRINKING BECAUSE . . .

 I'M GRATEFUL FOR . . .

1.

2.

3.

> Envision yourself fully present, creating
> a lifetime of memories you'll cherish.

 I PRACTICED SELF-CARE BY . . .

1.

2.

3.

 TODAY I ACCOMPLISHED . . .

 TOMORROW I WILL FOCUS ON . . .

☀ HOW I'M FEELING RIGHT NOW:

☀ TODAY I'M NOT DRINKING BECAUSE . . .

☀ I'M GRATEFUL FOR . . .

1.

2.

3.

> There's strength and courage in every challenge you face.

☾ I PRACTICED SELF-CARE BY . . .

1.

2.

3.

☾ TODAY I ACCOMPLISHED . . .

☾ TOMORROW I WILL FOCUS ON . . .

 HOW I'M FEELING RIGHT NOW:

 TODAY I'M NOT DRINKING BECAUSE . . .

 I'M GRATEFUL FOR . . .

1.

2.

3.

>>> Deep down you know when it's time to make a change
or leave an environment. Listen to the small whispers. <<<

(I PRACTICED SELF-CARE BY . . .

1.

2.

3.

(TODAY I ACCOMPLISHED . . .

(TOMORROW I WILL FOCUS ON . . .

☀ **HOW I'M FEELING RIGHT NOW:**

😃 🙂 😐 😔 🙁 😌 😍 😶 😣 😰 🙂

☀ **TODAY I'M NOT DRINKING BECAUSE . . .**

☀ **I'M GRATEFUL FOR . . .**

   1.

   2.

   3.

 If alcohol promises you confidence, connection, and less anxiety, ask yourself whether it's true and lasting.

☾ **I PRACTICED SELF-CARE BY . . .**

   1.

   2.

   3.

☾ **TODAY I ACCOMPLISHED . . .**

☾ **TOMORROW I WILL FOCUS ON . . .**

_____ / _____ / _____   _____ DAYS SOBER

 HOW I'M FEELING RIGHT NOW:

😀 🙂 😐 🙁 ☹️ 😌ᶻᶻ 😍 😕 😣 😖 🙂

☀ TODAY I'M NOT DRINKING BECAUSE . . .

☀ I'M GRATEFUL FOR . . .

1.

2.

3.

> It doesn't matter what you allowed in your past.
> Today is a new day that is yours to choose.

🌙 I PRACTICED SELF-CARE BY . . .

1.

2.

3.

🌙 TODAY I ACCOMPLISHED . . .

🌙 TOMORROW I WILL FOCUS ON . . .

_____ / _____ / _____   _____ DAYS SOBER

 HOW I'M FEELING RIGHT NOW:

😁 🙂 😐 🥲 😟 😴 😍 😕 😣 😖 🙂

 TODAY I'M NOT DRINKING BECAUSE . . .

 I'M GRATEFUL FOR . . .

1.

2.

3.

> You can get antioxidants (with no hangover!)
> from blueberries and chocolate.

 I PRACTICED SELF-CARE BY . . .

1.

2.

3.

 TODAY I ACCOMPLISHED . . .

 TOMORROW I WILL FOCUS ON . . .

KEYS TO SOBER GOALS

- Stay curious.
- Ask questions.
- Face your fears.
- Ditch what doesn't serve you.
- Fail forward.
- Seek clarity.
- Align with people who support you.
- Be gentle with yourself.
- _____
- _____
- _____
- _____
- _____

Anything else in your toolbox? Add it to the list.

☀ HOW I'M FEELING RIGHT NOW:

☀ TODAY I'M NOT DRINKING BECAUSE . . .

☀ I'M GRATEFUL FOR . . .

1.

2.

3.

> You are allowed to say no to anything that doesn't add value to your life without apologizing or overexplaining.

☾ I PRACTICED SELF-CARE BY . . .

1.

2.

3.

☾ TODAY I ACCOMPLISHED . . .

☾ TOMORROW I WILL FOCUS ON . . .

HOW I'M FEELING RIGHT NOW:

TODAY I'M NOT DRINKING BECAUSE . . .

I'M GRATEFUL FOR . . .

1.

2.

3.

> There is no perfect pathway to sober living—do the best you can for you.

 I PRACTICED SELF-CARE BY . . .

1.

2.

3.

TODAY I ACCOMPLISHED . . .

TOMORROW I WILL FOCUS ON . . .

☀ HOW I'M FEELING RIGHT NOW:

☀ TODAY I'M NOT DRINKING BECAUSE . . .

☀ I'M GRATEFUL FOR . . .

1.

2.

3.

> Celebrate (with zero-proof!) how comfortable
> you're becoming in your own skin.

☾ I PRACTICED SELF-CARE BY . . .

1.

2.

3.

☾ TODAY I ACCOMPLISHED . . .

☾ TOMORROW I WILL FOCUS ON . . .

_____ / _____ / _____   _____ DAYS SOBER

 HOW I'M FEELING RIGHT NOW:

TODAY I'M NOT DRINKING BECAUSE . . .

I'M GRATEFUL FOR . . .

1.

2.

3.

> People may judge you if you need to start over.
> Keep rooting for yourself because you haven't given up.

 I PRACTICED SELF-CARE BY . . .

1.

2.

3.

TODAY I ACCOMPLISHED . . .

TOMORROW I WILL FOCUS ON . . .

☀ HOW I'M FEELING RIGHT NOW:

☀ TODAY I'M NOT DRINKING BECAUSE . . .

☀ I'M GRATEFUL FOR . . .

1.

2.

3.

> Truth: Sober peeps are everywhere. Refuse to stay quiet to keep others comfortable; you'll miss out on connections.

☾ I PRACTICED SELF-CARE BY . . .

1.

2.

3.

☾ TODAY I ACCOMPLISHED . . .

☾ TOMORROW I WILL FOCUS ON . . .

 HOW I'M FEELING RIGHT NOW:

 TODAY I'M NOT DRINKING BECAUSE . . .

 I'M GRATEFUL FOR . . .

    1.

    2.

    3.

> Recognize with gratitude the chance
> you're taking on alcohol-free living.

 I PRACTICED SELF-CARE BY . . .

    1.

    2.

    3.

 TODAY I ACCOMPLISHED . . .

 TOMORROW I WILL FOCUS ON . . .

TWO SIDES TO SOBRIETY

Physical sobriety means to physically abstain from using drugs and alcohol. *Emotional* sobriety is the ability to recognize current feelings and be emotionally present after coming back from alcohol numbing your emotions. You are able to sit in your current feelings without judgment or trying to change them, knowing that no feeling lasts forever.

HOW DO YOU FEEL RIGHT NOW?

HOW INTENSE IS THE FEELING ON A SCALE OF 1 TO 10?

1   2   3   4   5   6   7   8   9   10

The longer you're alcohol-free, you'll notice the intensity of your feelings soften, as you also discover new ways to manage unpleasant emotions.

 _____ / _____ / _____   _____ DAYS SOBER

 HOW I'M FEELING RIGHT NOW:

 TODAY I'M NOT DRINKING BECAUSE . . .

 I'M GRATEFUL FOR . . .

   1.

   2.

   3.

>>> Never underestimate the power of a determined woman. <<<

☾ I PRACTICED SELF-CARE BY . . .

   1.

   2.

   3.

☾ TODAY I ACCOMPLISHED . . .

☾ TOMORROW I WILL FOCUS ON . . .

_____ / _____ / _____   _____ DAYS SOBER

 HOW I'M FEELING RIGHT NOW:

😃 🙂 😐 😔 😕 😌ᶻ 😍 😐 😠 😰 🙂

 TODAY I'M NOT DRINKING BECAUSE . . .

 I'M GRATEFUL FOR . . .

   1.

   2.

   3.

>>> Alcohol is not a staple and we can live healthy, fun, and beautiful lives without it. <<<

🌙 I PRACTICED SELF-CARE BY . . .

   1.

   2.

   3.

🌙 TODAY I ACCOMPLISHED . . .

🌙 TOMORROW I WILL FOCUS ON . . .

⭐ HOW I'M FEELING RIGHT NOW:

😄 🙂 😐 😔 😟 😴 😍 😕 😠 😖 🙂

⭐ TODAY I'M NOT DRINKING BECAUSE . . .

⭐ I'M GRATEFUL FOR . . .

1.

2.

3.

> The sober community has the most amazing individuals. Explore, reach out, and find your people.

🌙 I PRACTICED SELF-CARE BY . . .

1.

2.

3.

🌙 TODAY I ACCOMPLISHED . . .

🌙 TOMORROW I WILL FOCUS ON . . .

☀ **HOW I'M FEELING RIGHT NOW:**

☀ **TODAY I'M NOT DRINKING BECAUSE . . .**

☀ **I'M GRATEFUL FOR . . .**

1.

2.

3.

> Practice makes permanent, not perfect.
> Keep coming back to your intention.

☾ **I PRACTICED SELF-CARE BY . . .**

1.

2.

3.

☾ **TODAY I ACCOMPLISHED . . .**

☾ **TOMORROW I WILL FOCUS ON . . .**

☀ HOW I'M FEELING RIGHT NOW:

😁 🙂 😐 😢 ☹ 😴 😍 😕 😠 😖 🙂

☀ TODAY I'M NOT DRINKING BECAUSE . . .

☀ I'M GRATEFUL FOR . . .

1.

2.

3.

> Sobriety comes from within;
> it's the inner drive to do something for yourself.

☾ I PRACTICED SELF-CARE BY . . .

1.

2.

3.

☾ TODAY I ACCOMPLISHED . . .

☾ TOMORROW I WILL FOCUS ON . . .

☀ HOW I'M FEELING RIGHT NOW:

😄 🙂 😐 😢 🙁 😌 😍 😕 😠 😖 🙂

☀ TODAY I'M NOT DRINKING BECAUSE . . .

☀ I'M GRATEFUL FOR . . .

1.

2.

3.

> If you want to fly, give up everything
> that weighs you down.

☾ I PRACTICED SELF-CARE BY . . .

1.

2.

3.

☾ TODAY I ACCOMPLISHED . . .

☾ TOMORROW I WILL FOCUS ON . . .

_____ / _____ / _____   _____ DAYS SOBER

☀ HOW I'M FEELING RIGHT NOW:

😄 🙂 😐 😢 🙁 😌ᶻ 😍 😐 😠 😖 🙂

☀ TODAY I'M NOT DRINKING BECAUSE . . .

☀ I'M GRATEFUL FOR . . .

1.

2.

3.

>>> The only way to find your voice is to use it. <<<

☾ I PRACTICED SELF-CARE BY . . .

1.

2.

3.

☾ TODAY I ACCOMPLISHED . . .

☾ TOMORROW I WILL FOCUS ON . . .

_____ / _____ / _____   _____ **DAYS SOBER**

 HOW I'M FEELING RIGHT NOW:

😄 🙂 😐 😞 🙁 😌 😍 😶 😠 😰 🙂

 TODAY I'M NOT DRINKING BECAUSE . . .

 I'M GRATEFUL FOR . . .

    1.

    2.

    3.

> A relapse is never failure; it's feedback.
> Take the lessons and keep going.

☾ I PRACTICED SELF-CARE BY . . .

    1.

    2.

    3.

☾ TODAY I ACCOMPLISHED . . .

☾ TOMORROW I WILL FOCUS ON . . .

LET'S STOP GLORIFYING . . .

- Excessive drinking.
- Diet culture.
- Busyness and burnout as a badge of honor.
- Beauty standards.
- Numbers (on the scale, social media, and bank accounts).
- Strangers on the Internet behind filters.
- _____
- _____
- _____
- _____
- _____
- _____

What other societal expectations are silently destroying your spirit, confidence, and mental health? Add them to the list.

☀ HOW I'M FEELING RIGHT NOW:

☀ TODAY I'M NOT DRINKING BECAUSE . . .

☀ I'M GRATEFUL FOR . . .

    1.

    2.

    3.

≫≫   Drunk never looks good.   ≪≪

☾ I PRACTICED SELF-CARE BY . . .

    1.

    2.

    3.

☾ TODAY I ACCOMPLISHED . . .

☾ TOMORROW I WILL FOCUS ON . . .

 HOW I'M FEELING RIGHT NOW:

TODAY I'M NOT DRINKING BECAUSE . . .

 I'M GRATEFUL FOR . . .

1.

2.

3.

> You can do it—look the other way, keep scrolling, and stay in your own lane when excessive drinking is normalized.

I PRACTICED SELF-CARE BY . . .

1.

2.

3.

TODAY I ACCOMPLISHED . . .

TOMORROW I WILL FOCUS ON . . .

_____ / _____ / _____   _____ DAYS SOBER

☀ HOW I'M FEELING RIGHT NOW:

😊 🙂 😐 😢 😕 😴 😍 😶 😠 😖 🙂

☀ TODAY I'M NOT DRINKING BECAUSE . . .

☀ I'M GRATEFUL FOR . . .

   1.

   2.

   3.

The secret to happiness can be simple and sober.

☾ I PRACTICED SELF-CARE BY . . .

   1.

   2.

   3.

☾ TODAY I ACCOMPLISHED . . .

☾ TOMORROW I WILL FOCUS ON . . .

_____ / _____ / _____   _____ DAYS SOBER

☀ HOW I'M FEELING RIGHT NOW:

😄 🙂 😐 😢 🙁 😌ᶻᶻ 😍 😐 😮 😖 🙂

☀ TODAY I'M NOT DRINKING BECAUSE . . .

☀ I'M GRATEFUL FOR . . .

   1.

   2.

   3.

>>> Alcohol will never connect women authentically.
Build true community. <<<

☾ I PRACTICED SELF-CARE BY . . .

   1.

   2.

   3.

☾ TODAY I ACCOMPLISHED . . .

☾ TOMORROW I WILL FOCUS ON . . .

_____ / _____ / _____   _____ DAYS SOBER

★ HOW I'M FEELING RIGHT NOW:

😄 🙂 😐 😢 😕 😴 😍 😑 😠 😖 🙂

★ TODAY I'M NOT DRINKING BECAUSE . . .

★ I'M GRATEFUL FOR . . .

1.

2.

3.

 Together we can clear the path for anyone
who wants to live sober and free.

☾ I PRACTICED SELF-CARE BY . . .

1.

2.

3.

☾ TODAY I ACCOMPLISHED . . .

☾ TOMORROW I WILL FOCUS ON . . .

 HOW I'M FEELING RIGHT NOW:

 TODAY I'M NOT DRINKING BECAUSE . . .

I'M GRATEFUL FOR . . .

   1.

   2.

   3.

> Forget alcohol! Tell yourself what you really deserve is to discover new things and seek what truly matters in life.

I PRACTICED SELF-CARE BY . . .

   1.

   2.

   3.

TODAY I ACCOMPLISHED . . .

TOMORROW I WILL FOCUS ON . . .

☀ HOW I'M FEELING RIGHT NOW:

😁 🙂 😐 😢 🙁 😴 😍 😕 😬 😖 🙂

☀ TODAY I'M NOT DRINKING BECAUSE . . .

☀ I'M GRATEFUL FOR . . .

1.

2.

3.

>>>   We're here to experience life, not escape from it.   <<<

🌙 I PRACTICED SELF-CARE BY . . .

1.

2.

3.

🌙 TODAY I ACCOMPLISHED . . .

🌙 TOMORROW I WILL FOCUS ON . . .

 HOW I'M FEELING RIGHT NOW:

 TODAY I'M NOT DRINKING BECAUSE . . .

 I'M GRATEFUL FOR . . .

   1.

   2.

   3.

> You are absolutely capable of breaking the
> cycle of what no longer serves you.

 **I PRACTICED SELF-CARE BY . . .**

   1.

   2.

   3.

TODAY I ACCOMPLISHED . . .

TOMORROW I WILL FOCUS ON . . .

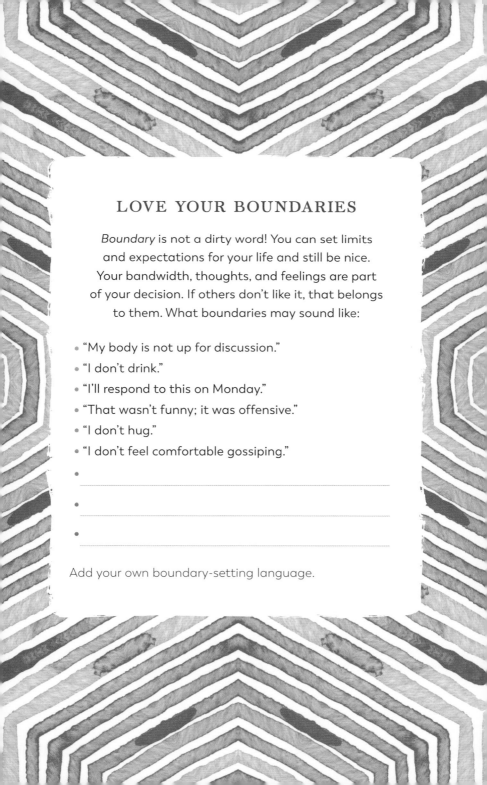

LOVE YOUR BOUNDARIES

Boundary is not a dirty word! You can set limits
and expectations for your life and still be nice.
Your bandwidth, thoughts, and feelings are part
of your decision. If others don't like it, that belongs
to them. What boundaries may sound like:

- "My body is not up for discussion."
- "I don't drink."
- "I'll respond to this on Monday."
- "That wasn't funny; it was offensive."
- "I don't hug."
- "I don't feel comfortable gossiping."
- _____
- _____
- _____

Add your own boundary-setting language.

_____ / _____ / _____   _____ DAYS SOBER

☀ HOW I'M FEELING RIGHT NOW:

😁 🙂 😐 😢 😟 😌 😍 😕 😠 😖 🙂

☀ TODAY I'M NOT DRINKING BECAUSE . . .

☀ I'M GRATEFUL FOR . . .

   1.

   2.

   3.

>>> Schedule in nonnegotiable time to take care of yourself. <<<

☽ I PRACTICED SELF-CARE BY . . .

   1.

   2.

   3.

☽ TODAY I ACCOMPLISHED . . .

☽ TOMORROW I WILL FOCUS ON . . .

☀ HOW I'M FEELING RIGHT NOW:

☀ TODAY I'M NOT DRINKING BECAUSE . . .

☀ I'M GRATEFUL FOR . . .

   1.

   2.

   3.

> When you take out alcohol, notice the space you have to be fully present in your life and in your emotions.

☾ I PRACTICED SELF-CARE BY . . .

   1.

   2.

   3.

☾ TODAY I ACCOMPLISHED . . .

☾ TOMORROW I WILL FOCUS ON . . .

☀ HOW I'M FEELING RIGHT NOW:

☀ TODAY I'M NOT DRINKING BECAUSE . . .

☀ I'M GRATEFUL FOR . . .

1.

2.

3.

> Stay connected, set reasonable expectations
> for yourself, and protect your peace and sobriety.

☾ I PRACTICED SELF-CARE BY . . .

1.

2.

3.

☾ TODAY I ACCOMPLISHED . . .

☾ TOMORROW I WILL FOCUS ON . . .

☀ HOW I'M FEELING RIGHT NOW:

😄 🙂 😐 😢 🙁 😌 😍 😶 😣 😖 🙂

☀ TODAY I'M NOT DRINKING BECAUSE . . .

☀ I'M GRATEFUL FOR . . .

1.

2.

3.

> There is no shame in doing
> what you need to do to feel better.

☾ I PRACTICED SELF-CARE BY . . .

1.

2.

3.

☾ TODAY I ACCOMPLISHED . . .

☾ TOMORROW I WILL FOCUS ON . . .

☀ HOW I'M FEELING RIGHT NOW:

☀ TODAY I'M NOT DRINKING BECAUSE . . .

☀ I'M GRATEFUL FOR . . .

1.

2.

3.

> Turn off notifications and ads, and unfollow or unfriend anyone who is not supporting your journey.

☾ I PRACTICED SELF-CARE BY . . .

1.

2.

3.

☾ TODAY I ACCOMPLISHED . . .

☾ TOMORROW I WILL FOCUS ON . . .

☀ HOW I'M FEELING RIGHT NOW:

☀ TODAY I'M NOT DRINKING BECAUSE . . .

☀ I'M GRATEFUL FOR . . .

1.

2.

3.

> You can create positive, energy-filled
> playlists that don't glorify booze.

☾ I PRACTICED SELF-CARE BY . . .

1.

2.

3.

☾ TODAY I ACCOMPLISHED . . .

☾ TOMORROW I WILL FOCUS ON . . .

☀ HOW I'M FEELING RIGHT NOW:

😁 🙂 😐 🙁 ☹ 😌ᶻ 😍 😐 😠 😖 🙂

☀ TODAY I'M NOT DRINKING BECAUSE . . .

☀ I'M GRATEFUL FOR . . .

    1.

    2.

    3.

>> Give your body all the good it deserves: nourishing food, hydration, movement, self-love, and preventive care. <<

 I PRACTICED SELF-CARE BY . . .

    1.

    2.

    3.

☾ TODAY I ACCOMPLISHED . . .

☾ TOMORROW I WILL FOCUS ON . . .

HOW I'M FEELING RIGHT NOW:

😄 🙂 😐 🙁 😕 😴 😍 😐 😣 😖 🙂

 TODAY I'M NOT DRINKING BECAUSE . . .

 I'M GRATEFUL FOR . . .

1.

2.

3.

>>> Alcohol will never taste as good
as living free and sober feels. <<<

🌙 I PRACTICED SELF-CARE BY . . .

1.

2.

3.

🌙 TODAY I ACCOMPLISHED . . .

🌙 TOMORROW I WILL FOCUS ON . . .

FROM THE AUTHOR

Six years ago, I made a choice to write and speak about my struggle with alcohol abuse. I wanted to raise awareness of the role I felt alcohol was playing in my life as a full-time working mom. Not a popular subject, I know, but a much needed one.

Within my social circle I didn't have any points of reference for what a non-drinking person looked like. Perhaps everyone knows someone impacted by alcohol, but we don't talk about it—not nearly as often as we should. I wanted to contribute to changing the narrative around normalizing sobriety. I haven't set the world on fire, but I've gained enough traction to know that I'm not alone in my feelings, experiences, and wishes for women to know they have other paths.

I am ready to receive all of the amazing experiences that lie on the sober path ahead of me. And if alcohol isn't adding value to your life, I invite you to find a new, alcohol-free path as well. Together, we can normalize sobriety as the healthy lifestyle choice it is. Rooting for you, always!

Michelle Smith

Recoveryisthenewblack.com

WHAT I'VE GAINED
IN SOBRIETY

- Boundaries
- Solid friendships
- Glowing skin
- Trust
- A bank account
- A clear conscience
- My life

WHAT YOU'VE GAINED SINCE
BEGINNING THIS JOURNAL

SOBRIETY RESOURCES

SUBSTANCE ABUSE AND MENTAL HEALTH SERVICES ADMINISTRATION (SAMHSA)

If you have questions but would like to remain anonymous, call SAMHSA 1-800-273-talk (8255). Trained professionals are equipped to provide information and resources.

@RECOVERYISTHENEWBLACK

Get regular Instagram inspiration from Michelle Smith, and come together with other women living or exploring an alcohol-free life.

SOBERMOMSQUAD.COM

Connect, share wins, tell life stories, and feel heard in a safe and supportive space. Inspiration on Instagram is free (@sobermomsquad); monthly paid membership unlocks a wealth of resources through the website.